HAIKU
inspiration

CHERYL ANTAO-XAVIER

All Rights Reserved. © 2021 Cheryl Antao-Xavier

Written by: Cheryl Antao-Xavier
Concept & Design: The Publishing Mentor / thepublishingmentor.com
Images: Pixabay / Canva, as credited
Cover Image: Canva

ISBN: 978-1-989403-30-3 [electronic book]
ISBN: 978-1-989403-31-0 [paperbook]
ISBN: 978-1-989403-32-7 [PDF]

Please address all copyright and reproduction queries to the publisher:
inourwords2008@gmail.com

Dedication: For Allan

Haiku is a short 17-syllable poem, traditionally arranged in three lines of 5-7-5 syllables. Haiku is oftentimes tied to themes of nature and the seasons.

The conventions around traditional haiku have loosened over the years with poets challenging the basics and experimenting with interesting variations.

In this book, I keep the haiku simple, using examples from nature and adhering to the syllabic count. Here is an example:

roses and jasmine	5 syllables
permeate the mourning soul	7 syllables
scents of love and death	5 syllables

Try writing your own haiku. For inspiration, look up images that inspire you and write your thoughts out. Come back to it and edit it into the syllabic count.

I hope you come to love this poetic form as much as I do.

Enjoy!

hope darkened by cloud
know the sun will rise again
wait for the clearing

sunlight through stained glass
turns the mood melancholic
recalling old times

IMAGE BY EVELINE DE BRUIN @ PIXABAY

dreams flit on light wings
skimming surfaces of life
tease reality

careless words pierce deep
weapons deadlier than most
wounds forever raw

IMAGE BY KEVIN MCIVER @ PIXABAY

to dust we return
some lie in peace, some restless
the ghosts of our past

IMAGE BY QLUG @ PIXABAY

darkness closes in
when spirits start to flicker
hell can be endless

roses and jasmine
permeate the mourning soul
scents of love and death

look not for storm clouds
eye draws what it wants to see
focus on fine day

IMAGE BY PUBLICDOMAINPICTURES @ PIXABAY

from bud to blossom
behold its time of glory
the first petal falls

change comes in due course
snow melts and fields come alive
with dancing daisies

IMAGE BY RUSTU BOZKUS @ PIXABAY

deep in the oceans
stirs the raging force unseen
a sunami birth

IMAGE BY PDPHOTOS @ PIXABAY

snowcaps start to melt
quietly through the balmy night
await the deluge

invasive species
silencing of the bulbul
echoes of lost song

IMAGE BY RAJESH BALOURIA @ PIXABAY

About

I am a poet who loves to pour thoughts into various poetic forms to hone craft and see what comes of it. I studied the ghazal in school, which should have put me off structured poetry for life, but when I came across haiku, I loved it immediately. I wrote some for fun, and am truly hooked.

Capturing a thought in a tight 5-7-5 haiku creates powerful missiles to aim at the big issues that trouble us...

Haiku Inspiration is the first in a series of thematic e-chapbooks. Do send in feedback. Thank you and enjoy!

Cheryl Antao-Xavier